D1724857

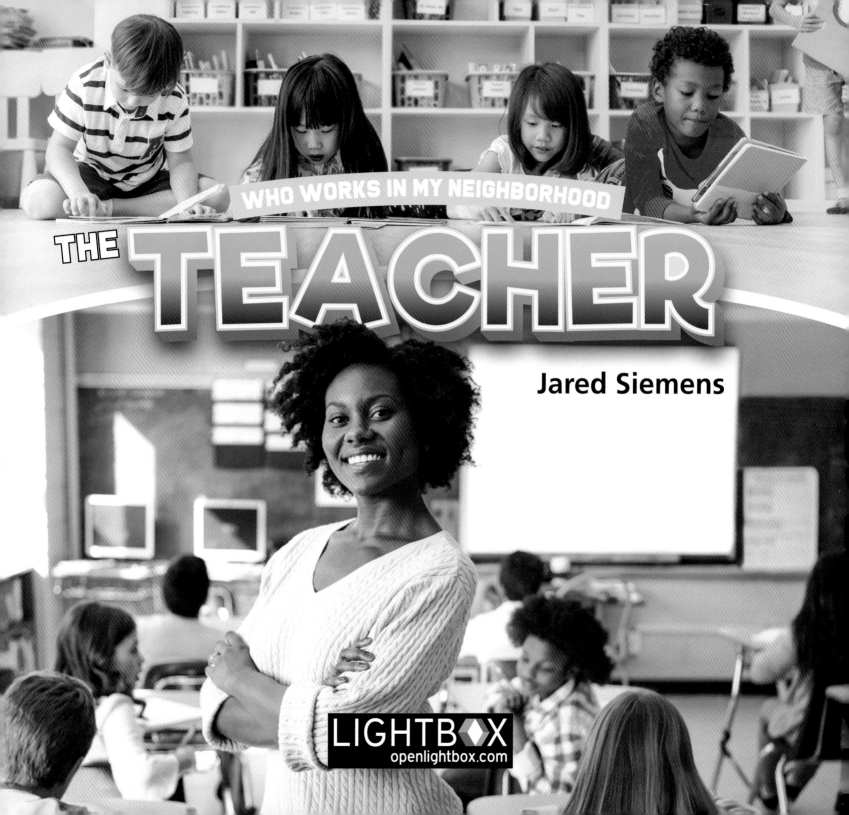

WHO WORKS IN MY NEIGHBORHOOD

THE TEACHER

Jared Siemens

LIGHTBOX
openlightbox.com

LIGHTBOX

Go to
www.openlightbox.com
and enter this book's
unique code.

ACCESS CODE

L B X Z 2 7 9 8

Lightbox is an all-inclusive digital solution for the teaching and learning of curriculum topics in an original, groundbreaking way. Lightbox is based on National Curriculum Standards.

OPTIMIZED FOR
✓ **TABLETS**
✓ **WHITEBOARDS**
✓ **COMPUTERS**
✓ **AND MUCH MORE!**

2

Copyright © 2021 Smartbook Media Inc. All rights reserved.

STANDARD FEATURES OF LIGHTBOX

AUDIO High-quality narration using text-to-speech system

VIDEOS Embedded high-definition video clips

ACTIVITIES Printable PDFs that can be emailed and graded

WEBLINKS Curated links to external, child-safe resources

SLIDESHOWS Pictorial overviews of key concepts

INTERACTIVE MAPS Interactive maps and aerial satellite imagery

QUIZZES Ten multiple choice questions that are automatically graded and emailed for teacher assessment

KEY WORDS Matching key concepts to their definitions

VIDEOS

WEBLINKS

SLIDESHOWS

QUIZZES

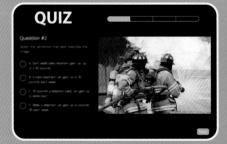

THE TEACHER

Contents

3

The teacher is a person in my neighborhood.

4

A teacher works at a school.

The **Mather School** in Boston, Massachusetts, is more than **375 years old**.

Teachers help children learn new things.

More than **50 million children** attend public school in the **United States**.

The teacher shows me how to read, write, and count.

She tells me about places in the world.

11

My teacher helps me use books and computers to learn.

There are about **90,000 elementary schools** in the United States.

13

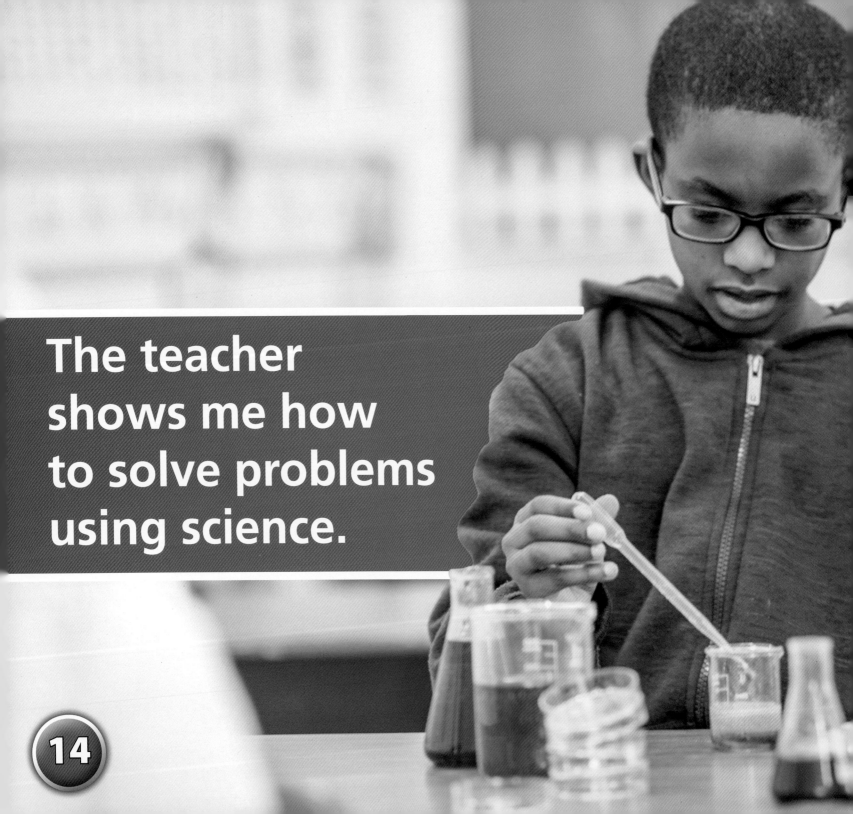

The teacher shows me how to solve problems using science.

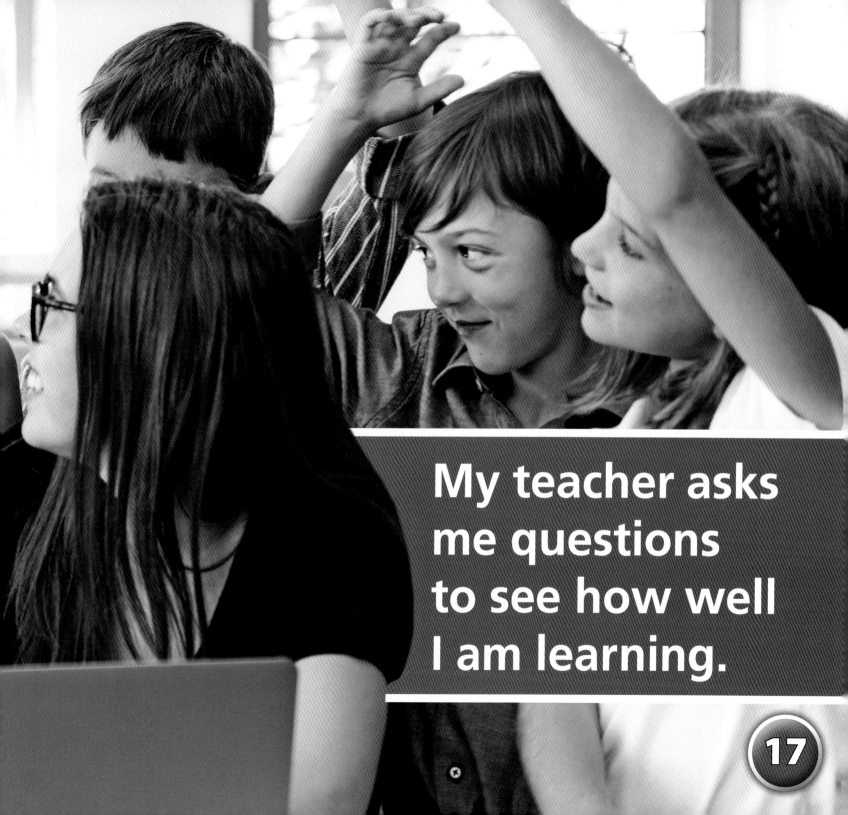

My teacher asks me questions to see how well I am learning.

17

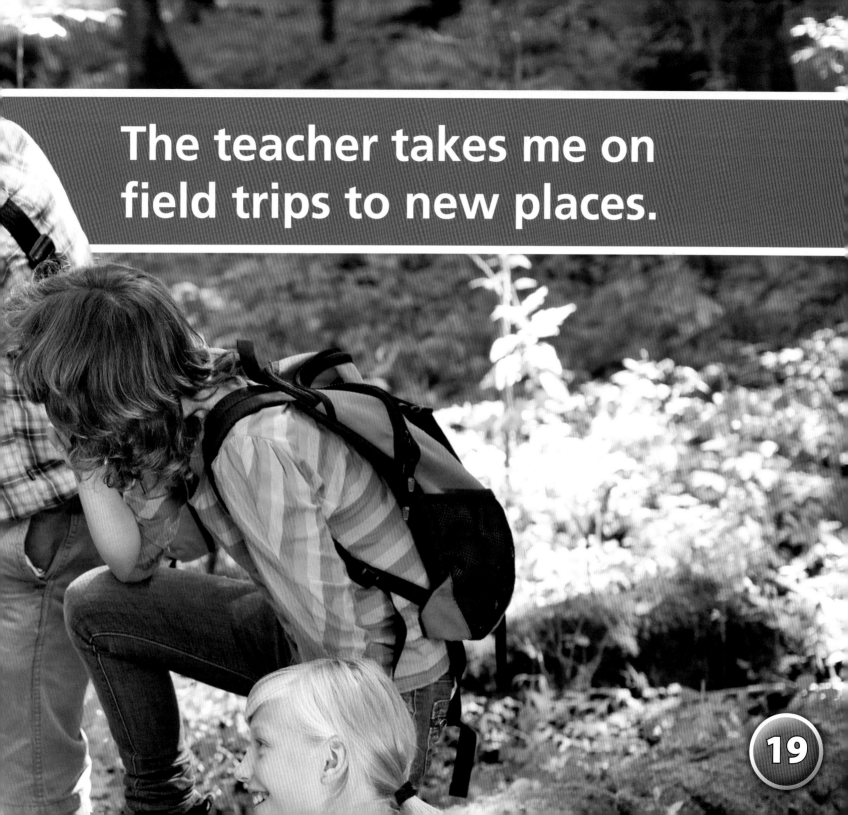

The teacher takes me on field trips to new places.

19

Teachers are important people in my neighborhood.

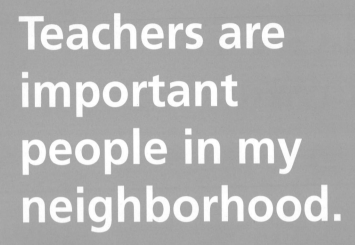

There are about **1.6 million** kindergarten and elementary school teachers in the United States.

See what you have learned about the teacher.

Describe what you see in each of the pictures.

KEY WORDS

Research has shown that as much as 65 percent of all written material published in English is made up of 300 words. These 300 words cannot be taught using pictures or learned by sounding them out. They must be recognized by sight. This book contains 44 common sight words to help young readers improve their reading fluency and comprehension. This book also teaches young readers several important content words, such as proper nouns. These words are paired with pictures to aid in learning and improve understanding.

Page	Sight Words First Appearance	Page	Content Words First Appearance
4	a, in, is, my, the	4	neighborhood, person, teacher
7	at, more, old, school, than, works, years	7	Boston, Massachusetts, Mather School
8	children, help, learn, new, states, things	8	public school, United States
10	and, how, me, read, shows, to, write	10	count
11	about, places, she, tells, world	13	computers, elementary schools
13	are, books, there, use	14	problems, science
17	am, asks, I, see, well	17	questions
19	on, takes, us	19	field trips
20	important, people	20	kindergarten

Published by Smartbook Media Inc.
350 5th Avenue, 59th Floor, New York, NY 10118
Website: www.openlightbox.com

Printed in Guangzhou, China
1 2 3 4 5 6 7 8 9 0   24 23 22 21 20

042020
110819

Project Coordinator: Ryan Smith
Designer: Ana María Vidal

Copyright ©2021 Smartbook Media Inc.
All rights reserved. No part of this publication may be reproduced, stored in a retrieval system, or transmitted in any form or by any means, electronic, mechanical, photocopying, recording, or otherwise, without the prior written permission of the publisher.

Library of Congress Control Number: 2020934520

ISBN 978-1-5105-5359-0 (hardcover)
ISBN 978-1-5105-5360-6 (multi-user eBook)

Every reasonable effort has been made to trace ownership and to obtain permission to reprint copyright material. The publisher would be pleased to have any errors or omissions brought to its attention so that they may be corrected in subsequent printings.

The publisher acknowledges Getty Images, iStock, and Wikimedia Commons as the primary image suppliers for this title.